111 WAYS TO FINDING YOUR SOUL'S PURPOSE

Chelsea Winton

Copyright © 2024 by Chelsea Winton
All rights reserved.

Table of Contents

Introduction	v
Dedication	vii
Number 1	1
Number 2	2
Number 3	3
Number 4	4
Number 5	5
Number 6	6
Number 7	7
Number 8	9
Number 9	10
Number 10	11
Number 11	12
Number 12	13
Number 13	14
Number 14	15
Number 15	16
Number 16	17
Number 17	18
Number 18	19
Number 19	20
Number 20	21
Number 21	23
Number 22	24
Number 23	25
Number 24	26
Number 25	27

Number 26	28
Number 27	29
Number 28	30
Number 29	31
Number 30	32
Number 31	33
Number 32	34
Number 33	35
Number 34	37
Number 35	38
Number 36	39
Number 37	40
Number 38	41
Number 39	42
Number 40	43
Number 41	44
Number 42	45
Number 43	46
Number 44	47
Number 45	48
Number 46	49
Number 47	50
Number 48	51
Number 49	52
Number 50	53
Number 51	54
Number 52	55
Number 53	56
Number 54	57

Number 55	58
Number 56	59
Number 57	60
Number 58	61
Number 59	62
Number 60	64
Number 61	65
Number 62	66
Number 63	67
Number 64	68
Number 65	69
Number 66	70
Number 67	71
Number 68	72
Number 69	73
Number 70	74
Number 71	75
Number 72	77
Number 73	78
Number 74	79
Number 75	80
Number 76	81
Number 77	82
Number 78	83
Number 79	84
Number 80	85
Number 81	86
Number 82	87
Number 83	88

Number 84	89
Number 85	90
Number 86	91
Number 87	92
Number 88	93
Number 89	95
Number 90	96
Number 91	97
Number 92	98
Number 93	99
Number 94	100
Number 95	101
Number 96	102
Number 97	103
Number 98	104
Number 99	105
Number 100	106
Number 101	107
Number 102	108
Number 103	109
Number 104	110
Number 105	111
Number 106	112
Number 107	113
Number 108	114
Number 109	116
Number 110	117
Number 111	118

Introduction

I want to give significant consideration in this book to the most charming and magical creature that I can think of, and that is the firefly. They naturally light their way as they go from place to place, and they come equipped with their own light.

I feel fireflies are beacons of hope, illuminating the darkness and reminding us that hope prevails even in the darkest times. Their dance of illumination can be seen wherever they go on their path. Their synchronized dance symbolizes harmony and unity, emphasizing the importance of living in harmony with nature and each other. We do not come equipped with our own light. Often, light sprouts from the depths of darkness. We all have the light within us. It is up to us to turn it on and make it shine as brightly as we can. We must shine with all that we are in this lifetime.

This book will help you find your soul's purpose and path in life. Every single one of us is born with a purpose and gifts that we need to live our lives. We need to learn lessons in order to discover these gifts and bring them to fruition. There are many ways that you can help yourself do this. It mostly starts with going within, listening, and being somewhat in solitude so that you can hear clearly what will be coming to you. This book goes over many ways—111 ways, to be exact. There are many more ways to help yourself reveal your soul's purpose and life's journey as everyone is completely different and uniquely wonderful.

I use the symbol of fireflies for my book as I think they are dancing little lights of joy and miracles within themselves. As I said, you have to go within to see your light. Well, these beautiful little creatures already have their light lit within as they are born this way. They are an example of chatoyancy at its finest and in the most spectacular form—a diaphanous glow of pale gold coming from within to light their journey. I think they are extraordinarily special and unique and give me a wonderfully beautiful insight into why I wanted to create this book. I found freedom within myself and from loving myself.

I once believed my body was a cage until the day I let my soul sing and be free. You can do the same . . . Free your soul by going within and loving yourself more than anything else.

Dedication

I dedicate this book to my son. I wish him to fulfill his life's purpose and soul's path. I know his journey will be incredible. He is my son, and I am extremely proud of him. I know that he will find his way. I have great confidence in him. I hope this book helps him if he needs it one day. I will always be here to help him do anything that fulfills his life's purpose in the best way possible.

I also dedicate this book to the love of my life—yet to be determined and found, but you already are my hero. Maybe I've met you before, or maybe I haven't met you yet. I know you exist, and knowing this has helped me in so many ways to go within and search my heart and soul, thus being able to find my own soul's purpose—to let out what has been there all along.

It is with their love that writing this book has been possible.

We must not have fear in seeking our soul's mission. When we have fear, we stand still. We should just lose our fear and go forward on our journey. There is nothing to fear but fear itself. FEAR has two meanings: (1) "forget everything and run" and (2) "face everything and rise."

The choice is yours. The choice is always yours, and you must choose yourself without the limitations of fear. Face everything and rise. Rise to your soul's purpose. I believe in you.

Number 1

The number one way you can find your purpose is by becoming pure of heart and emptying out the heartbreak and anything you harbor in your heart that keeps you from going forward and moving on in your life's journey. This is the number one step to make it possible to find out your life's and soul's purpose. Having a pure and open heart is your first step into becoming all that has been envisioned for you since birth. You are the precipice of greatness. Do not stop now! Do not ever stop with the progression of your soul's journey. The pain we have endured in life to date does not compare to the love, joy, and peace of what's to come. Trust and believe me as it is true.

Number 2

You must let go of anything that no longer serves you in your life. You must let go of anyone or anything that brings any amount of pain to your heart and soul. Let it go . . . You cannot hold on to the past to go forward. It weighs you down and slows you down from becoming the next highest version of yourself. Let it all go! However, how that looks can differ from person to person. There's no wrong way to do it, so be gentle with yourself. Whether it's writing it down and burning it or it's writing it down and putting it in a jar until the jar is full and then burning all of it at once—get rid of it all!

Number 3

When seeking out what your soul's purpose is, you must also be in a state of open-mindedness. You must listen carefully and closely, and you must go places where there is a lot of quiet to the point where you feel like you're seeking solitude for yourself. Being in solitude is not a punishment—it's a luxury. When you think of it that way, you are never actually alone because you're always with yourself. All you need to be complete is yourself. We are born alone, and we die alone. Remember that, and you will never ever feel alone again because you always have yourself. You are the only person that you will have your entire life. So count on you and listen to your soul. Once you know you have and love yourself, you find happiness in yourself instead of all these other empty places where people usually look for happiness outside of themselves. People look for happiness in wealth, cars, jobs, other people, and trips. All these materialistic things will not bring you true happiness. Your soul's purpose will reveal itself very soon when you can find true love and happiness within yourself. Don't ever underestimate the power of loving yourself.

Number 4

You must always look within yourself to find your path and your purpose. This is why you were created in the first place. What you choose to do was possibly defined even before you came here to earth. But you must return to calm. You must sit and listen quietly—whether it's meditating in nature, being surrounded by animals, or wherever that is for you. Find that location and be grateful for it. Visit it or recreate it often and thank that spot for creating a safe place for you to figure out what it is you were meant to do and why you are here. Everyone has a life purpose, why they are here, and gifts that they need to unfold right before their very eyes. Failure is the greatest teacher. Through failure, we always learn a lesson, and we learn to try again. Failure is never to be treated as a mistake. There are no mistakes in life—only lessons. In these lessons, we discover our soul's purpose.

Number 5

Choosing to love yourself every single day and before anything else is how you can help yourself and others the most. Choosing yourself is basically the same as choosing others as well. Let me explain this further. When you choose yourself, you fill your cup first, and you look after you. This allows you to look after others as well. So this shows you how important it is to always choose yourself and love yourself the most. Choosing yourself and loving yourself ultimately leads you to finding your soul's purpose as it opens your heart and starts your heart on the course of becoming pure. Sacrifice and sacredness go hand in hand. Sometimes we have to surrender and release one thing in order to get what is meant for us and what is sacred to us. Sit with yourself and listen to the dulcet tones of your soul calling to you, telling you what to do next and what it longs for the most. Your soul knows what it wants and how to get it. You must be open enough to listen and follow the intuition of your soul. It is never wrong. When people ignore their soul's calling, they do the greatest disservice for themselves as human beings. They will never create their truest and most authentic selves doing this. They end up living a very false existence. This will never lead you to your soul's purpose.

Number 6

When trying to find your path, do not give in to fear. Fear leads to darkness and then anger, then hate. Then it equates to suffering. You only have fear in fear itself. Don't let fear exist. There is nothing to fear but fear itself. Your focus determines your reality. Do not give any light to the darkness. Always focus on what your heart desires. This will lead you on the right path to your soul's purpose. Be loyal. Try to be a cynosure wherever you go. This is done by consistently being all these things in your life without fail. Do this through actions, not just words, as actions speak far louder than words ever will.

Number 7

In order to find your path and to have it show itself to you, you must be observant rather than demanding. You must see what's around you. You must be quiet. You must be still, and you must observe with all your might. Demanding outcomes and predetermining how things should go will never happen for you or how things will unfold naturally. Your light, your path, your destiny, your soul's purpose will show itself when you observe and be still and quiet in everything around you. You must listen. Remember again you must listen to the quiet, and in stillness is where we heal. There will not be any human voice, but you must listen, and you'll be shown the way. In tranquility is when we hear the most.

Do you realize that pouring all your love and effort into your person will make all your dreams come true? Many people don't seem to realize this, but whatever you show the world the universe gives you back tenfold. Show as much love as you can to your loved ones, and everything will boomerang back to you in every possible way for your life. You will flourish in every way possible, and when you flourish, your path becomes clearer. How wonderful it is to just love as much as you possibly can to fulfill your dreams! What a beautiful world we live in. I love the word "sonder," and I feel it applies to us in our journey. It's the realization that each passerby has a life as vivid and complex as our own. Each person has a soul's purpose and dream to fulfill. We must do all we can to bring it into reality. Do not ever underestimate the power of love. With the power of love, anything is possible—you can bring anything into your life through love.

Number 8

You can also find your way on your journey and eventually to your soul's and life's purpose through mistakes. Don't ever regret trying and making a mistake as it will teach you a lesson and propel you forward in life. Your mistakes will eventually lead you to discovering the truth. Please always have the resilience and grace to continue on even if you make mistakes more than once as mistakes are where the greatest lessons in life are learned. I can't stress this enough. If you never make a mistake, you never learn anything new. You stay stagnant and complacent in life. Never quit trying to fulfill your desires and wants. You need to be in the state of mind that what you want wants you more, what you desire desires you more, and what you seek is already seeking you. Never show a state of lack to the universe. This is always going to keep you from obtaining your needs, heart's desires, and, furthermore, happiness.

Number 9

When your intentions are pure, remember you will never lose. You may lose people. You may lose other things. But if they don't understand that your intentions are pure, they may not understand you, and that is okay. Not everyone is meant to understand why we do the things we do. The things we do have been programmed since birth. They are not us. They don't walk in our shoes, and they do not live our lives. Don't ever expect everyone to fully understand you. Still be you and do what you need to do to discover your journey and your path in life. It's just that it's your path and your journey. Claim them for yourself. You are the only one that can.

Number 10

The universe will always replace what exits your life with something bigger and better. Don't be stuck holding on to the past or resisting change. Welcome new energy. Let go of what needs to be removed so you can gain clarity in your direction.

There are great blessings in surrendering and allowing, not in resisting and living in the past potential outcomes. Let go of expectations and allow what is meant to be for you.

Number 11

Who you surround yourself with matters.

This year, I want you to surround yourself with the best people. The right people. Your soul tribe. Those that match your energy and vibration. Those that lift you up. Those that make you smile, laugh, and feel safe. Those people that are always cheering for you even when you're not in the room—especially then! Surround yourself with people that can't wait to see you and you can't wait to see. That let you be you—all of you! That celebrate you and cheer you on. Surround yourself with people that simply make you feel good and have your back without fail. These people will help you find your true destiny in this world. They make you strong and resilient on your journey. We all need our people around us. No one thrives alone. You must realize the power of resiliency as without resiliency, we would never have the strength to move forward on our soul's path.

Number 12

You don't realize how strong you are until you look back at everything you've overcome. Life has been creating you for what you are meant for and what you were born to be. We all have a divine purpose here on earth. It was chosen for us before we came here. We all have gifts to unwrap within ourselves. Let's be present in order to unwrap our presents meant to grace this world. Our gifts are instilled in us to make this earth we call home a better place. The gifts are here within us to make heaven on earth. Now you understand the importance of unveiling these wonderful gifts that are in you and have been in you all along for you to discover.

Number 13

This is the year you realize that everything you've been wanting has been yours all along. You already have everything you need in your complete self. It is the year you manifest your dreams by accepting them within you. You must look within as this is when you also awaken, and your path will magically appear right before your eyes. Look within yourself, and you will see clarity in your life's journey and vision. The exigent and imminent importance of you going within yourself cannot be overstated enough. You must go within to reveal the answers to your soul's desires and, furthermore, purpose. What will you do right now to start? Whatever comes first to mind is absolutely perfectly right for you to do at this moment. So go do it now—the power of now!

Number 14

Surrender everything to the universe about any expectations of outcomes that you desire.

Author Eric John Campbell says, "Surrender everything that has to do with how you'll achieve your dream life and trust that your intuitive, natural impulses will know what to do in each moment." You do know what to do for your soul's purpose. So trust yourself and always move forward. Never pause and go backward—you aren't going that way. Trust that the universe has a far better plan than you could've ever imagined for yourself. Trust it, and it will be.

Number 15

Sometimes things happen before you are ready for them to happen. It doesn't mean that the timing is wrong. Sometimes it means that the timing is just right and that the universe knows you are ready and maybe just needed that extra push in the right direction to get you on your way.

Embrace this new journey with everything you are. Everything is unfolding exactly how it's supposed to, even if you can't see it like that just yet. Every moment of the day, wherever you are is exactly where you were meant to be. Nothing is by coincidence. Nothing is by accident. Everything happens just as it should, and absolutely everything has a reason for it.

Number 16

You are one thing only. You are a divine human being—an all-powerful creator of your own reality and destiny. You are a vessel; and inside of you dwells the infinite wisdom of the ages and the sacred creative force of *all* that is, will be, and ever was. You are unique and rare with your own spirit and talents given just to you. You need to release these talents, and in return, you will flourish in all you do and seek in life. So in this very moment, go and be your creator of your life, journey, and soul's purpose. You must pay attention to things that matter the most to you. Reflect on the things that you care about and bring zest to your life. Give those things the attention that they deserve as they are the key to why you are here. Recognize your strengths and talents as those are given to you for a reason, and you must uncover that reason. No two humans are exactly the same, and this is for a reason. We all have incredibly different purposes and lessons for our soul. So do not ever compare yourself to another as there is no one else just like you.

Number 17

The most beautiful souls are the ones that have known struggle, bleakness, defeat, heartbreak, suffering, and loss but have found their way out of the darkness. It is in darkness that light is born and blooms in all its glory. Through that pain is growth, courage, and wisdom to go toward the light and your pathway. Remember that having courage is wisdom, and having wisdom is in turn courage. You must find the courage deep within yourself to always move forward on your life's journey or path no matter what is thrown at you in life. Life is not always easy, but we must prevail. Nothing of magnificence is ever easy.

Number 18

I want you to notice what brings you genuine happiness, the kind that seeps into your core, giving you hope and a sense of purpose. I want you to pay attention to all the laughter and smiles in your life and delve into what captivates and challenges you, sparking a desire to learn and grow. I want you to zero in on what makes your heart and soul feel like home. When you do this, you align yourself with your greatest, highest self, and soul's purpose. Pay close attention to all the beautiful moments around you. They are abundant and simple. They are everywhere. The more beauty you see naturally, the more beauty lies within yourself. You are beautiful, and you are magic. Now go see it in all you do. It is everywhere to discover once you truly can see. Open your eyes!

Number 19

Don't ever give up on what you believe in. When you give up on your beliefs, your intuition, and what your soul is trying to tell you, you give up on everything that you've done to date—making it all for nothing. Once you believe in something, you must always believe in it and not give up on bringing it into your life. This cannot be your reality . . . so don't let it be. Don't give up on your dreams, or your dreams will give up on you. Don't let your dreams become walls. Giving up on your dreams is the greatest service to oneself and to becoming your true, authentic self. We all have dreams in our hearts, and they never ever would've been planted there if they were not meant to come to fruition. You must always devote yourself to your dreams. Thoughts become things. Also, be very careful what you feed your mind. Feed your mind with positivity, joy, and love. It's much like feeding your body: If you feed your body with bad food, you feel bad. If you feed your body with good, healthy food, you glow and feel good. This is how your mind works as well. It is very much the same, so be very careful what you tell yourself. Your thoughts and words are incredibly powerful and thus influence your life.

Number 20

Happiness can lead to fulfillment and your heart's desires. Be happy on purpose.

Go outside, run, walk, move, smile, and stretch that body. You are made to move.

Read a book. Call a friend.

Meditate. Write in a journal.

Drink water. Eat good food.

Breathe. Learn something new. Express gratitude.

Chase the sun. Dance.

Create magic. Be in love. Sing, pray, wish, sit in silence. Filling your soul with love and joy will lead you to where you need to be. Live like there is no tomorrow as it is never promised. There is a strange amount of serendipity that plays into finding one's soul's purpose. I believe this to a fault. Go be happy now and do whatever comes to mind. Do it well and often. Go put on your favorite song and dance for three minutes straight and see how happy you are after. I bet you'll have a smile on your face. I think you have one now. You are a powerful being.

Number 21

Fear is only powerful if you allow it to be. Be brave. Conquer the day with me by your side! Let's use this day like no other! Let's go forward! Let's do everything in our power to make our path as clear as day to us. Be mindful, be joyful, be present, be patient, be kind, be all the goodness in your heart to the point where your heart becomes pure. With a pure heart, you will find your soul's purpose. It's you and yours alone to discover all for your glorious self. It's all there right in front of you. You just have to go get it and decide that you're making it so. Then it will be! What is your soul's purpose? You are about to find out, love. You are about to find out . . . I am so excited for you. You have no idea! Go now, my sweet soul.

Number 22

You need to love yourself first as that is who you will be spending the rest of your life with guaranteed. No one else in your life is guaranteed to be with you your whole life. Always choose yourself and always love yourself first. This is not egotistical at all. This is a necessity for you to discover the true, authentic, and highest version of yourself—the self that is meant to do all that was envisioned for you and what you were meant to do here on earth. Loving yourself unconditionally will lead you to your soul's purpose.

Number 23

You will learn more on bad days than good days. You will learn more from pain than joy. This is how you obtain growth. You have to focus more on the growth rather than the setbacks. Everything that happens to you comes with a lesson. It is up to you how you view each thing that happens to you. If you view it as necessary for growth to put you on the path farther down your journey to enlightenment and finding your soul's purpose, then each setback is well worth it. A "setback" is exactly what it says: set it back where it belongs—in the past—and go forward. I believe in you!

Number 24

The more grateful and thankful you are, the more you attract things to be thankful for. You must always be in a state of gratitude. Be grateful for everything you have right now because you have everything you need right now. You will always have everything you need within yourself when you're in a state of gratefulness and thankfulness. Gratitude is a way for you to appreciate what you have instead of always reaching for something new in the hope it will make you happier or thinking you can't feel satisfied until every physical and material need is met. Gratitude helps you refocus on what you have instead of what you lack. Never be in a state of lacking or wanting. You must be in a state of having, being, and doing. This is what continues you on your path. If you act as if you have everything your heart desires, then there is no choice for the universe but to make your heart's desires a reality. You will find your soul's purpose in a state of never lacking anything. You always have everything you need within you.

Number 25

One thing you can do right now that will greatly improve the clarity that you will see going forward in the direction of your divine destined path is to cleanse all your spaces: your home, your bedroom, your car, your garage, your heart, your mind, and, yes, even your beautiful soul. Literally everything needs to be rejuvenated and cleared. New things are about to start coming into your life, so make sure you are properly welcoming them. Make space for everything you deserve and desire in life. Clutter and stagnancy lead to the mind being stuck in the very same way. Remember our surroundings are us.

The old saying "You are what you eat" is true for the mind as well. As I have said before, you are what you think, surround yourself with, and feed your mind, heart, and soul. Let the soul be free to find its purpose.

Number 26

Don't ever be afraid to be alone. To be alone isn't a punishment. It is a time to self-reflect, heal, and learn to be happy with just yourself. When you master this, you will start to unfold the gifts that you have as well as your purpose or what you are meant to do here on this earth. Being alone is never a punishment. It is actually something to relish in and to be grateful for. In my self-isolation, which I chose to do, I began to become my true, authentic self. This was when I started to realize which things in my past no longer served me and let them go. And how to do just that will differ for each person. We will have different ways of doing these things, so there is no right or wrong way. Just listen to the intuition of your soul. Your soul will tell you what you need to do. I needed to just be alone, with my own thoughts and my own company. You must learn to love yourself as you are actually the love of your life. Of course, we all long for and wish for a great love. But remember you are truly the love of your life.

Number 27

I totally get that we all have days when we just want to rest, relax, and not think about pursuing anything other than relaxation. It is good for us to turn our mind off and rejuvenate and reset. But when your game is back on again, make sure you get up, show up, dress up, and never ever give up. We all have times when we feel worn down as we are human. We just want to rest—this is also the time that we heal. We heal in silence, so being quiet and restful is good for you. You need to do that, and you deserve it, so don't ever feel guilty about it. But when it's time to get up and show up again, let's do it! Let's find our divine purpose. Rejuvenating is resiliency. You are resilient and able to do anything you put your mind to.

Number 28

Please don't let anyone dim the sparkle that you have within you. What you have within you is your true, raw power. Never let that be diminished by anyone or anything. Your sparkle and joy are exactly where your power lies. This is why it is so important to not let anything dim that beautiful sparkle.

We all have spiritual love in us. This can refer to love rooted in a spiritual connection that helps us find meaning and purpose in our lives. Follow that spiritual love and sparkle and let it light your way on your path.

Number 29

When you possess a million-dollar vision, avoid surrounding yourself with individuals who have a ten-dollar budget for their vision. Come out from among the ordinary and strive for the stars, where you belong as you are a star finding its way—its way to a higher state and vibration. This will lead you to your soul's purpose and the gifts within you.

Here are ten ways to raise your vibration:

1. Connect with nature and animals.
2. Listen to binaural beats and happy music to keep you calm.
3. Practice gratitude.
4. Raise the vibration in your most frequently visited and favorite spaces.
5. Think joyfully and positively.
6. Focus on areas of your life that need improvement.
7. Focus on what you love the most.
8. Cut out things that weigh you down.
9. Be in the moment of now.
10. Don't worry and stress—this brings you only more strife in life.

Number 30

In your spiritual life, you need to not react to obtrusive things around you.

To be calm, cool, and wise is the greatest asset in the world. When we are calm, time stops. There is no time. Karma stops. Everything stops.

Everything becomes null and void. In this state is where clarity is born. You need as much clarity and calm as you can. This will allow your soul's purpose to emerge and present itself to you. Do whatever you can to keep yourself calm and remain that way no matter what life throws at you. This can be very difficult at times, but I have faith in you, and you can do it.

Number 31

Below is one of the most beautiful quotes. I love Rumi immensely for his many wise poems and words. Follow his wise words and gain courage, for courage is wisdom, and having courage feeds your soul, thus aiding you in finding your soul's divine purpose.

> Oh soul,
> you worry too much.
> You have seen your own strength.
> You have seen your own beauty.
> You have seen your golden wings.
> Of anything less, why do you worry?
> You are in truth
> the soul, of the soul, of the soul.
>
> —Rumi

Number 32

Mindfulness isn't about erasing thoughts—it's about being at peace with them.

Stay positive. Stay focused on creating positive new thoughts and energy. Train your mind to remain positive even when negative thoughts or emotions come up. It's all how you view each thought, viewing it as a lesson good or bad. All lessons in life are required for your path and mean something. Try to be at peace with all your thoughts as thoughts are things. The mind is very powerful. Be careful what you tell it and what you believe. Your mind needs to be in a positive state in order to find your path and journey in life. A negative mind leads you astray and away from your soul's purpose.

Number 33

I need you to pause for a moment . . .

Pause now . . .

Unclench your jaw.

Soften your forehead.

Drop your shoulders.

Blink your eyes.

Sink into the chair and take three deep breaths.

Repeat until you feel comfortable within your body. Then listen and ask the questions you want answers to deep within your soul. Ask for clarity and ask to be shown how you can help yourself discover your purpose in life. Ask, why am I here? What am I meant to do? Then listen and pay attention to how your body, mind, and soul feel. Whatever comes to mind, go and do it—and do it to the best of your ability. See what happens and what becomes clear to you. Keep doing whatever it is as your path will slowly reveal itself to you. Come back to your truth and center. Call your power back and remember who you are. You are a very powerful person, and you must realize that. There is only one of you for a reason. You are here with a divine purpose. We all are . . .

Number 34

You must not grieve everything that is lost in your life as I believe that it will always be replaced with something better. I don't mean replacing people or pets—I mean your lost life experiences. They will always be replaced with something better—something that is meant for you. Something that is meant for you will always find you, and you must have faith. Without faith, you have nothing; and with faith, you have everything. Your path and purpose will always find you if you look for them and seek them. You must desire them and not give up. Like any great desire and love in life, it must be fed your attention and energy in order to succeed.

Number 35

Synchronicity is all around you. This can involve seeing numbers, signs, and all kinds of things that give you a feeling of not being alone. Tune in to it and pay attention to what is being shown to you. Synchronicities can remind us that we aren't alone—we are connected, and there is a mysterious and meaningful direction to our lives. We meet strangers (who might feel like angels in disguise) in unexpected circumstances who offer us the exact words or experience we need at that precise moment. These are all synchronously timed in our lives.

Things are showing signs of coming together. You are getting in alignment and enlightenment.

Keep going—you're on the right path to finding your way. Pay close attention to what is being shown to you. Be present and aware, and your path will show itself.

Number 36

Let me assure you that you already have all you need inside you. You are complete as you are now. You just need to discover it.

You are worthy of all the blessings. You are worthy of being adored and loved. You deserve all the abundance in the world to flow easily and effortlessly to you. You deserve prosperity just as you are right now, in this exact moment. The divine *loves* you, and in their eyes, you are already *perfect*! You were perfectly placed on this earth to fulfill all that was envisioned for you before you came to earth. So quit sitting there reading my book and get out there and discover all that is yours to behold and fulfill your soul's calling.

Number 37

I believe that your path is more difficult because your calling is higher. You are anointed and special. You were a creation out of love, and you are love. You are a one and only. There is only one of you out of over 8 billion on this planet, Earth. That is irreplaceable, and so are you.

Make your journey happen. Make it come to light. Make it your reality.

Shock everyone and show them what you are made of and just how amazing you truly are. Make me proud of you . . . Actually, I already am. Go to an idyllic place or have an experience that is extremely pleasant, beautiful, or peaceful and sit with yourself. You—yes, you—are an amazing creation. Sit with yourself and listen to the music your soul will sing to you. Nothing truly divine ever comes easily, nor should it as it is a path that many detour from because it is easier. Please don't ever do that as you mean too much to this world to choose easy and effortless.

Number 38

You must believe in yourself no matter what negative chatter may come from your mind.

Believe in what your heart desires and knows to be what you need. Believe in it until it manifests for you. Don't overthink it. Just believe in it and allow it. Never give up on what your heart knows and desires. It is never wrong. Being true to your heart will lead you to where you need to go on your journey. The heart and soul know the way. Trust them and go for it.

Number 39

Make sure you have integrity in all you say and do. What you project to the world comes back to you. This is very powerful, and every intention leads to an outcome. What you say matters. Your words are only as powerful as the actions they precede. When you don't follow through, you rob them of any value.

Don't tell people what they want to hear. Don't live in the sad, artificial world of unfulfilled commitment. Don't create an illusion of your intent. Fulfill it through accomplishing goals and accepting consequences. Your responsibilities won't go away. When you choose to avoid them, you bar yourself from ever enjoying the area of your life that they occupy. You rob yourself of continuing down the destined path of where you are meant to go and be. When you have integrity in all you do, you have motion to find your soul's purpose. We all have setbacks, but let these be only an ephemeral moment in time. They too shall pass. Then forge on.

Number 40

I want you to think about your worth. Do you realize how much you are worth? Loving yourself and choosing yourself will lead you to finding your worth. There are people that don't think they are worthy and deserving of good things in this life. The universe will mirror that back to them, saying, "This is what you're asking for. So here you go." It's wild that when you decide you're worth more, the universe starts opening doors to make it a reality. When this happens for you, what will follow is a clear, fulgent light of direction to your soul's purpose. You are worthy, deserving, and good enough right now as you are, my dear. You must believe that!

Number 41

Your soul already knows and holds all the answers you need. You just have to be quiet enough to hear it and brave enough to listen. Are you brave enough to hear what your soul will say? Speak less, listen more, react less, and observe more. Do some introspection. Introspection is perhaps one of the best ways to discover and search your soul. Soul-searching is "the process of figuring out your purpose, your motivations, and what may need to change in your life in order to live in greater alignment with your true self." Don't be afraid. Be very excited for what's next as change is growth and progress. You are on your way, my dear.

Number 42

The longest journey you will ever take is the distance from your head to your heart. Your heart and head will constantly be at war with each other. It is important to be rational and sensible, but it is also important to listen to your heart because your heart's intuition is fed from your soul deep within. Those that go within become awakened to their soul's purpose.

Number 43

Remember, before every miracle is delivered to you, there are major breakdowns before you have major breakthroughs. Every storm is followed by a sunny, blue day. We need the storm to clear out of our way everything that no longer serves us so that we can see the miracle that is in front of us. We need to open our eyes and see what is all around us. Sometimes we are so closed off that we can't see something that is right in front of us. Signs from the universe can be showing us the way to our soul's purpose, but we can be blind to it if we don't tread carefully with eyes open on this journey.

Number 44

Let's do something fun today. Share the best lesson that you've ever learned in your life with one of your friends. Pick up the phone now and call someone and tell them the best lesson that you've learned in life. This will also give someone else the gift of what you've learned. Then ask them the same question: "What is the best lesson that life has given you?" See what they have to say. We can learn something here. When we speak, we discuss what we already know. But when we listen, we learn something new. I will tell you the greatest lesson that life has ever taught me. It is experiencing true romantic heartbreak. As painful as it was, it taught me so many lessons, and it caused me to rise up and become stronger and better than ever before. That heartbreak is what is responsible for actually leading me to my soul's purpose. My soul's purpose is to spread unconditional love to as many people as I can. It is to help them to discover their soul's purpose and in turn create betterment for the entire earth. Heaven on earth is my deepest wish and greatest heart's desire.

Number 45

Do you know what makes you truly happy? This seems like a very simple, straightforward question, but many people do not know the answer to this. If someone asked you, this answer should roll off your tongue immediately. It isn't something you should even need to think about. What makes you truly happy? What is your greatest heart's desire? What is your truest fulfillment in life? What do you need to do right now to make these things a reality? Whatever the answers are to these questions, I suggest you do them and do them as soon as you can. Tomorrow isn't promised. So what are you waiting for? Let's head down the path to your enlightenment and your soul's purpose. What are the answers you are seeking to make yourself truly happy?

Number 46

What also will propel you on your way to your soul's purpose is finding what you're truly passionate about. What are you truly passionate about? What makes you excited? What makes you have a drive without having to feel like you're working—something that you love and care about so much that doing it is seemingly effortless? What is that passion in you? Do you know? If not, you must seek it from within and discover it. We are all uniquely different, and our passion will be something different from someone else's. Discovering your passion can be one of the most liberating things in life. Fulfilling that passion is what sets you free and lets your soul feel like it's on fire with a passion that is intended just for you.

Number 47

In this journey, we also have to discover what eats at us. We also need to be good at following and honoring ourselves with the best of intentions always. What keeps us awake at night? What haunts us? What causes us trauma? What has caused us trauma in the past? No matter what issues we are dealing with, we need to find the resolve to find solutions for them and heal from them. Healing is something that never ends in life. It is ongoing—you can't do it wrong. You can't speed it along. You just need to look after yourself and do what's right to help yourself with letting these things go. They don't need to live in us. They have had a place in our life as it is part of our journey, but they don't need to stay there. They've served their purpose, and they can leave now. Things that cause us distress and hurt are going to slow us down in discovering our soul's purpose. So we need to wipe these from us clear, clean, and away at all costs. They no longer serve us. They do not define us by any means. We are not a product of what has happened to us. It's very possible that during this, you will be happy, hurting, and healing all at the same time. This is progress. This is good. Keep going, my dearest soul.

Number 48

They say a person needs just three things to be truly happy in this world: (1) someone to love, (2) something to do, and (3) something to hope for. Is this true for you? Do you have all three of these things? If you do not, you need to try to seek these out to fulfill your heart's desires and soul's purpose. I've said this before, but you must often be reminded to say to yourself and the universe, "What I seek seeks me more. What I desire desires me more. What I want wants me more." Now see what happens and what the universe sends and gives you. You must believe you are worthy, deserving, and good enough to have it all right now because, let me assure you, you are! Also, remember you always have everything you need for anything you want at any given moment. You are always complete. No one or nothing completes you.

Number 49

Let's try this today. It's what I call "shower meditation."

Shower meditation involves this: Every time you take a shower, visualize washing away your stress and anxiety down the drain, never to return. Concentrate on the feeling of the water upon your skin, slowly washing away all that no longer serves you. Envision the power of the water washing away your negative thoughts and feelings. Feel sadness, betrayal, grief, regret, anger, heartbreak, and depression being washed right off you. Let it all go down the drain. You'll start to feel lighter and much clearer in your journey. Then finish with a blast of as cold of water as you can stand for thirty seconds. It will rejuvenate everything in you. As you've just flushed everything holding you back off your body, you are free to carry on clean, healthy, and refreshed.

Number 50

Your entire life can really change in a year . . . You just have to love yourself enough to know you deserve more, be brave enough to demand more, and be disciplined enough to actually work for more. I absolutely know this to be true. I know that a year sounds like a long time, but so much can happen in a year. It is all absolutely amazing. It can be astounding. If you believe, if you do the work, and if you try to fulfill what your heart's calling is. I am a completely different person from what I was a year ago, and I do believe I am becoming the highest version of myself. It's a never-ending journey. Transcending and ascending never stop in this lifetime. But we can continue to carry on and move upward always. That is all we can ever do. Don't ever let yourself down. You are the most important person to yourself and the only person you will be with your entire lifetime. Do not ever let yourself down.

Number 51

Stop stressing please! If you are struggling or stressing, you must find a way to stop. Yes, I know this is only very easy for someone to say, but actually very hard to do. I understand. But if you can stop yourself from struggling or stressing, which is deemed to be of a negative mindset, then you will be doing yourself the greatest favor. If you ask yourself, "Will whatever that is making me struggle and stress matter in a year?" If the answer is no, then don't give it another thought of worry. It doesn't deserve that energy. All you ever have is now. So if you're present enough in the now, stop stressing, stop struggling, and just be more joyful and replace the worry with anything other than a negative emotion. Whatever that looks like for you, please try to do it and do it daily and do it often. This will train your mind to not instinctively go first to a place of worry and struggle.

You must believe with all your heart that something big is about to happen to you. At the right time, the universe will give you what is yours. This is fact. This is absolute, and it will happen for you, I promise. Once it does and you live life like this, just watch your soul's purpose reveal itself to you. You are so strong, and you are so powerful—remember that.

Number 52

Remember nothing will ever be the same after this moment, this day, this week, this month, and this year. Time never repeats itself. Remember how valuable your time is. Your time is very, very valuable. It is incredibly valuable. You must realize this! You must think this way and realize that every precious moment of your life is never to be repeated again.

Nothing will be the same after any amount of time has passed. Mentally, physically, spiritually, and energetically, you will be entering a new day, a new world, a new life, a new way, and a new path. You are awakening to your soul's purpose, my dear. What are you going to do in this very moment that's going to change your life, even if it's a very small thing and seems very trivial to you? Believe me, it is not—no moment is trivial or meaningless. I want to know at this very moment, what is it? Tell me now!

Number 53

Did you know that there are two people inside of everyone? There is the king or queen that you were meant to be, and then there is a fool. Each of these can come up and show itself in different ways and not be steadfast. What you have to learn is this: be honorable and have that king or queen that you were meant and born to be as the only one that appears. Cast that fool aside, never to return. Be with people that speak only to your king or queen. Don't be with anyone that speaks to you as a fool because you are not a fool. You are a king or queen, and you have been predestined and were born to be that king or queen—always! A fool will always be tricked into the wrong path. Never be a fool, not even for one precious moment of your time.

Number 54

One thing we can all work on is setting boundaries. It is always okay to explain your boundaries to another person. It is not okay to try to convince someone that you are worthy of these boundaries. If you have to do that, then you are enabling a losing battle. If they can't see your worth and honor your requirements for setting boundaries that keep you safe and in turn keep them a part of your life, then you may have to revisit your relationship with them. I believe that anything that you ever have to try to convince someone of is basically a losing battle as they are never going to hear you. If you are trying to convince them but they don't hear you or listen to you and honor what you're saying, then it isn't your concern any longer. Remember what someone else thinks of you is never your business. Have you ever had an epiphany? It's a moment when you suddenly feel that you understand or become conscious of something that is very important to you. What anyone else thinks just doesn't matter because it never matters what someone else thinks of you. They have not walked in your shoes, and they have not been subject to your life experiences. They have no right to judge you based on their lives. This is very powerful and something you must realize and live by.

Number 55

I want you to think about this and see if you've ignored things in the past. I bet you have—we all have. I know I sure have. It's about listening to our gut when it comes to detecting and identifying red flags, which present themselves in things of this world or in people we know. You must trust your gut instinct as it is always right. It is a form of protecting you. When we choose to ignore these red flags, we do harm to ourselves. We also enable the things and people in this world that are willing to do this to others, allowing them to continue. Let's stop this one thing or one person at a time and not ignore red flags. I used to ignore red flags to the point that they were waving banners, and I would grab them and wrap them around my neck like a scarf. All kidding aside, I always wanted to see the best in people, and I always gave them the grace of an excuse as to what their behavior was truly telling me. Do not ever ignore your gut instinct. It will help you on your path to your soul's purpose. You must learn to always trust yourself and to never question your gut. When you get to this point, you will realize how helpful this is for you and your journey. Don't ever ignore the incandescent beam that is lighting your path and calling to you. It is also called your "intuition" and your "soul's course." Your soul knows, and your intuition knows—never doubt either. They are always right.

Number 56

I believe that possessing humbleness, forgiveness, clarity, love, courage, and wisdom is the way to an awakened soul. You need to flush the *E* out of "ego" and go!

Ego death is "the disappearance of an individual's sense of self, or the removal of one's perception of oneself as an entity separate from one's social or physical environment." Your ego keeps you weak and longing. Your ego must die for you to be reborn and to realize your soul's purpose. You are not your conditioned ego. You are so much more.

Number 57

I want you to take pleasure in the simple things: sitting by a stream, watching a butterfly flutter in the garden, watching the sunset, the sunrise, the stars, the energy in the moon—anything that's free and beautiful and ever changing and never the same way twice. It's in the simple things that we actually find the most pleasure. But in today's society, we seem to forget that. For me, it's enjoying a full moon—just me out on my patio, looking up at it and the beautiful pool of light that it sheds on me. I enjoy it immensely. I think I especially enjoy it because the moon is out when things are calm, dark, and quiet. There are very few people relishing its energy at any given moment. That's what makes it so special for me. I feel as if it's shining only on me at that moment. I enjoy it as it is the simplest of things, but it brings me peace and happiness, and that means the most to me. Find that for you. The simplest of things can bring us so much calm, peace, joy, and happiness—like the cup of coffee you have in the morning. How do you like your coffee? It can be so simple and yet provide profound enjoyment. Make sure you have the simple things exactly the way you like them best and relish in the simplicity of each moment you enjoy them. Going back to the basics is where you will find your soul's path.

Number 58

What we can also do to help ourselves is just take one day at a time. If we look ahead to our whole journey and our whole life, it will seem ominous and never ending and that we're constantly searching for our path. Don't search for it or chase it. You just have to be in a state of faith where it's going to present itself to you. Just slow down. Take one day at a time. Remember, short steps, long vision.

Number 59

If you continue each day not choosing for yourself, the world and the universe will choose for you. Do not let other people choose for you. Do not let others decide your fate. You have to show up each and every day and put effort into choosing for yourself. You have the power and strength to decide and choose for yourself. You must trust in yourself, your intuition, and the divine. When you trust yourself implicitly, you are on your way to finding your soul's purpose. This doesn't happen overnight, of course. But with consistent work and effort, this will become a natural way of being for you. You will have the desire to choose for yourself. You will know that no one else can choose better for you than yourself. No one wants to spend their life trying to fit in a box that someone else has determined right for them. You deserve better. Decide right now that you are in charge of you and you alone. Do not ever live your life for someone else. This is living falsely, and you will continue down the wrong path and never find the path meant for you. It is hard to truly value others if you don't value yourself. So changing your mindset to value yourself and to always choose for yourself helps others and helps the world as a whole become a better place down the road. One person at a time. This is possible and will happen. Start the chain reaction, start the ripple effect, and start today. It can all start with you, my dear.

Number 60

Do this today and keep it up. Decluttering our stuff also declutters our mind. It lessons anxiety and stress as well. If our space is clean and free of clutter, our mind feels the same and can then process and create new thoughts and things clearly. It will make you feel happy and light.

Cleanse all your spaces: your home, your room, your car, your heart, your mind—everything. They say cleanliness is next to godliness. New things are about to start coming into your life. So make sure you are properly welcoming them. Will you be ready? Get ready now!

Number 61

Do yourself a favor and do these things for yourself. They are more in depth than what we already spoke about setting boundaries and such. They are more detailed things that you need to do for yourself to become clear and present so that your path can become clear and present itself to you.

You can be a kind, loving, caring, compassionate, and considerate person yet still do the following:

- Say no (for your well-being)
- Prioritize your needs
- Set boundaries
- Disagree with people if it is not your belief
- Be honest and to the point.
- Challenge poor behavior
- Walk away from toxic environments
- Make mistakes (as we learn from them)
- Stand up for yourself
- Protect your time, energy, and space

You must do these for yourself as no one else will do them for you!

Number 62

Be the person you would like someone to be for you. I like the saying "Be the person your dog thinks you are." Get up early so you can get that second cup of coffee before work.

Pick yourself back up when you fall down or make mistakes. Be soft and kind and guide your gentle heart out of the dark places your mind and ego like to take you to, which wastes time.

Stop waiting for the next best thing—that job, house, or relationship—to appear in your life before you start truly living it. Your time is now! Stop waiting for things to happen. Live now and make them happen for yourself!

Number 63

Some of the kindest souls I know have lived in a world that was not so kind to them, yet they live and talk to others in pure eloquence. Some of the best human beings I know have been through so much at the hands of others, but they still love and care deeply. Sometimes it's the people who have been hurt the most who refuse to be hardened in this world because they would never want to make another person feel the same way they once felt. If that isn't something to be in awe of, then I don't know what is. I have experienced this personally, and I will never let it change my heart and soul. Keep true to yourself, and you will always prevail on your soul's journey. It's when you derail yourself from your authentic self that you get lost. Be in the euphoria of knowing you are on the right path. You are always right where you need to be in this universe. Never second-guess that there's a reason for everything.

Number 64

Be brave! Protect that beautiful heart of yours! We are the only ones that can protect our heart. We can't trust anyone else to do it for us.

I think it is incredibly brave the way you look for the light even when the darkness feels overwhelming. Always remember to look for the light. Like I said before, light is created from darkness.

"As water reflects the face, so one's life reflects the heart" (Proverbs 27:19). "Guard your heart above all else, for it determines the course of your life" (Proverbs 4:23).

Number 65

Say this as soon as you wake up and before your feet hit the floor. Set an intention for the day. Be grateful for the day before it even starts. Expect miracles, blessings, kindness, and love; and then you will receive them. Your day will go however you've predetermined it to be.

I have the power within me to create the life I desire.
I choose to let go of fear and doubts and take inspired action.
I see possibilities where others see obstacles.
I am capable of achieving anything I set my mind to.
The universe always provides everything I need.

I start the day in gratitude for my life. Always live in a state of gratitude as you always have something to be grateful for. When you are in a state of gratitude and are grateful for everything that you have in the present moment, the universe will see this and give you more to be grateful for. Gratefulness will lead you to your soul's path.

Number 66

I absolutely love the way the sun dances on water. It looks like glimmering diamonds. It also presents to me all the infinite possibilities of glimmers of hope. It's truly stunning to see, and I stare at it for as long as I can every time. It lets me imagine that I can manifest anything my heart desires because I can, and so can you.

Glimmers are those mini moments in your day that make you feel joy, happiness, peace, or gratitude. Once you train your brain to be on the lookout for glimmers, these tiny moments will begin to appear more often in your life. It can be so beautiful to become very aware of the tiny glimmers of things in life that most people overlook. Be aware, and you will see things unfold right before your eyes. The eyes are the window to the soul. Your eyes see everything, but do you? Open your heart, mind, and soul. Your eyes will follow suit, and you will see the beauty in everything.

Number 67

It is very important to know that the journey of healing is never ending. Being always happy and joyful is not something you have to constantly do or have at the forefront of your mind as it is not realistic. There are many emotions for us to feel and be real with.

Healing doesn't mean you'll always feel joy. It means that when you face tough times or sadness, you have the experience and understanding to manage your feelings and get back to a balanced state. It's about coping and adapting, not constant happiness—this is unrealistic. Being realistic with yourself also keeps you true to yourself, and you honor yourself, which in turn will keep you on your soul's journey. Before I lean toward sounding loquacious, I must say again that there is nothing more important than staying true to yourself, your heart, and your soul.

Number 68

Let yourself be happy! This next chapter in life is called "You deserve this." It's your turn, my dear.

Life hasn't always been easy, and you have made some mistakes, but you ended up here for a reason.

We are all learning how to live correctly and appreciate why we never got what we thought we deserved in the past. When we don't get the things that we thought we deserved in life, we must realize that we weren't rejected—we were redirected!

So when you do feel happy, let yourself be happy.

You deserve all the blessings that are coming to you!

Just realize these blessings are sometimes in a disguise that only you and your heart and soul will recognize.

Number 69

Be so calm about finding your path that it ends up working itself out. Sometimes you just need to surrender and enter the trusting phase to allow things to come together for you. When you are calm and worry-free and just surrender and trust the process, the universe will unfold as it is meant for you. That is how you can be trusting enough to let your soul find its way. Your soul knows the way home. We all long for home. I know I do. Go home—it's where you belong, my dearest.

Number 70

And then, finally, it happens . . .

One day, you wake up, and you're in this place.

You're in this place where everything feels right.

Your heart is calm. Your soul is lit. Your thoughts are positive. Your vision is clear. Your faith is stronger than ever. And you're at peace—at peace with where you've been, at peace with what you've been through, and at peace with where you're headed . . . You are on your way! When you wake up and feel this, realizing that you are truly on your way to your soul's purpose, it is the most wonderful feeling you can ever feel. Rejoice in it and recognize it when it's happening and give it the gratitude it deserves. It is why you are here on earth. You are magnificent, so believe it.

Number 71

I read this and loved it! It's true: we always have a choice, and we are in charge of our decisions and our own reality. Let's always choose wisely for ourselves.

"Sad" has three letters, but so does "joy."

"Fall" has four letters, but so does "rise."

"Curse" has five letters, but so does "bless."

"Ignore" has six letters, but so does "listen."

"Enemies" has seven letters, but so does "friends."

"Immature" has eight letters, but so does "maturity."

"Ignorance" has nine letters, but so does "knowledge."

"Negativity" has ten letters, but so does "positivity."

You always have two realities to choose from in life.

It's up to you to decide which one you want to live your life. It's always up to you how you choose to live your life and how to honor the desires of your heart, soul, and destiny.

Number 72

Honor change and don't be afraid of change.

You can literally feel in your soul when it's *time*: time to move on from people, time to make a change in your life, time to get rid of unhealthy habits, time to want *more* for yourself. At some point, you'll just know. Your soul knows . . . You must listen and always trust your soul's intuition. It's never wrong. With change comes progress, and with progress comes growth, and with growth, we become stronger and better than ever before. Be strong, be powerful, and be wise. You are that king or queen in you, not a fool.

Number 73

Let yourself shift! We are constantly in a change of shifting our energies. Let this flow. Let it be natural. Let everything come and go as it pleases. It's like a leaf floating down a stream—it's at the mercy of the path of the stream, and it just goes with it. Do not fight anything. When you fight or chase something, it will always be at a distance from you. It's when you surrender, trust, and let everything go and flow that everything will happen for you.

As you are shifting, you will begin to realize that you are not the same person you used to be. The things you used to tolerate have now become intolerable. Where you once remained quiet, you are now speaking your truth. Where you once battled and argued, you are now choosing to remain silent. You are beginning to understand the value of your voice and that there are some situations that no longer deserve your time, energy, and focus. You must save your voice for those that will hear it and for those who will honor your sacredness.

Number 74

Let's revisit this and be very clear with what kind of life you want. Your mind is very powerful, and you become the intentions that you set and what you think about.

Decide what kind of life you really want. Then say no to everything that isn't that. You have the power and right to say no!

Never apologize for being very clear and set in your intentions of what you want and where you're going. No one else is on your path or journey; and they don't have to understand it, like it, or even approve of it. All you have to do is know that you're doing the best for you and that it is what you truly desire. It is your life and your life alone. It is your path and your path alone. We are the only person that we are with our entire life. So we are in charge of ourselves and our soul's journey. Never apologize for being your true, authentic self—not ever!

Number 75

There is something else we can do for ourselves: Do not run with the pack. Do not be like everyone else. Do not follow everyone else's lead and become comfortable conforming to society's expectations. Come out from among them. Travel the path less traveled. Go your own way. Go your own direction. Do not follow others. You must be the leader of your soul's journey. Be a leader, not a follower. Remember a lion does not care about the opinions of sheep. Come out from among the common. You are anything, but common. Be the brightest shining star among the millions—the star that lights the way to your path and destiny.

Number 76

Let's think about this: You know that the sun cannot grow a plant that's already dead or that water has no effect on fake flowers. Think about everything that is actually realistic and what can actually help you. Sometimes the things that we think helps us in life or helps us grow actually don't. We think that buying things or doing other meaningless things in the moment fills a void or fills our moments and is helpful to us. But actually, it isn't and is meaningless. Let's fill our moments with things that are meaningful and progress us forward. Let's fulfill our greatest heart's desires and go toward them. Be mindful of where your time and energy go and do not squander them. They're precious and valuable. It's your direction and pathway. Ask yourself what would help you right now at this moment. Then go do it!

Number 77

Let's make this the standard in our everyday life: always be the better person.

You must make your intentions pure, led by your heart.

What and who you are is what you'll attract. Pain is inevitable, and it will always exist. But if you focus on understanding what you are feeling and why you are feeling it, you will overcome it. Let it go, and this too shall pass. Learning to let go is one of the hardest things that we will ever have to master in our lifetime. But I promise you this: if you can do it, you can do anything, and you can have anything that your heart desires. Don't ever give up and don't give up on your path.

Number 78

Seriously, I'm not trying to beat a dead horse, but this is such an important lesson to learn and master. I'm sorry if you find things redundant in this book, but I am seriously just trying to hammer this home. We must learn to do this masterfully.

You must learn to let go of things that no longer serve you and decide you want a good life. The universe will start moving things to make it happen. The people you need will appear. You will find your soul tribe and vibe. The healing you need will happen. The doors you need open will open. Once you truly and sincerely decide you are worthy, miracles will flood in. You are worthy of all seeds that have been planted in your heart, and you already have everything you need within you to make it happen. Believe me!

Number 79

How nice it is to think of that we've all had wonderful moments in our life and wonderful days and memories. But remember that some of the best times of your life haven't even happened yet. Truly, this is a magical truth, and it's for you to discover. Be excited for tomorrow, the day after that, and every other day to follow the rest of your life on your soul's journey. Get excited as you have every reason in the world to be excited. No two days are exactly the same. Remember the next one can always be better than the last. It's up to you!

Number 80

The most rewarding thing you can do for yourself is to take the chance. The only thing we ever regret in life is not doing something. You'll never regret taking the bull by the horns and making the choice to go and try. Try everything in your life that you want to accomplish. Sometimes you will fail, and sometimes you will succeed. Neither one of those is the point. The point is that you tried and never gave up.

Your comfort zone is where the brilliance of your potential is held captive. It confines you within its walls, limiting the expansiveness of your human spirit. Every chance you take will bring you one step closer to your dream life and your greatest heart's desires. Fear will always be there, driven by the ego. But it's up to us whether we want to listen to it. Living in fear is not living. In fear, all you ever have to fear is fear itself. Once you realize that, you can conquer anything. Fear keeps you stagnant and frozen in place. Don't ever live in fear. It's an illusion that you put in place for yourself. Fear is only an illusion that you have created in your mind. Once you realize this, you'll know anything is possible.

Number 81

You can't see the next chapter of your life if you keep your focus on reading the last chapter over and over again.

Let that sink in for a minute. Now read it again. You will never progress this way. Something that is in the past needs to remain in the past because it's just that—in the past. It's already happened. You can't change it. The outcome will never be different. You just have to move on and create the future to be unlike the past. Don't repeat old cycles—things that you keep doing over and over—and expect a different outcome. They were lessons you should've learned from. Now let's not repeat them again. There's no time to waste anymore. Move on to the next wonderful chapter of your life. It's all waiting for you to discover. Let's go find it and turn that page, one page at a time.

Number 82

Just in case someone hasn't told you this yet today, go to the mirror and tell this to yourself often. Do it every day!

You are more than enough! You are so very loved and valuable. There is only one of you, so this makes you incredibly rare and worthy. You are good enough for all you desire right now. Not in a week, not in a month, not in a year—right now! Go grab all you deserve and do it to the best of your ability.

Number 83

In the midst of life's chaos and challenges, never forget this: you absolutely deserve happiness, love, peace, joy, better days, and a beautiful life.

Keep going, keep improving, and keep shining. Light that magnificent, fulgent light within and light the way home. You know the way, and you have the power and potential to find it. This comes from within your soul, so listen closely.

Number 84

I love this . . . Stay focused and on your *P*s: prayer, priorities, peace, positivity, patience, and, most important of all, your path. If you do this faithfully, you will receive blessings and glory in your future.

Number 85

Let's remember we are human, and we all make mistakes. I've talked about this before, and a mistake is better because it teaches us a lesson, unlike not doing anything at all.

A mistake repeated more than once is a decision.

A mistake repeated more than twice is a habit.

A mistake repeated more than thrice is a character.

Don't repeat a mistake! Learning from it is part of growing. Repeating it is wasting your time and energy. Don't waste your time and energy. They are far too valuable to you. Your time and energy are what makes you . . . you. And as I said before, you are far too valuable to waste.

Number 86

Believe in yourself and the journey you are on. It is important to acknowledge your accomplishments no matter how small they may seem. Every step you take, every obstacle you overcome is a victory. Remember that success is not a destination, but a journey. Keep going my dear. Your journey never ends.

Number 87

You need to be the magic and most likely are without even realizing it.

But you have to be a magician. You have to make the magic happen. Real magic is not about gaining power over others—it's about gaining power over yourself. Remember that you are divine.

Be patient. Remember patience is one of the greatest virtues. Nothing of value ever comes from rushing.

Number 88

Ten steps to protect your vibe and bring forth your tribe:

1. Avoid gossip and drama as they're negative.
2. Let go of things you can't control. You will just drive yourself crazy.
3. Avoid comparing yourself to others. We are all different people.
4. Keep your faith larger than your fears. Faith is huge. Fear is small.
5. Don't do anything that doesn't feel right. You know by feeling it.
6. Don't be afraid to spend some time alone. It's not a punishment. It's a luxury you find yourself in when alone. You heal in silence.
7. Speak softly and kindly to yourself and other people. You will always get a more positive response.
8. Please yourself before trying to please others. Remember you cannot please everyone, so stop trying.

9. Stay away from people who drain your energy. Becoming exhausted can happen to you, so avoid this at all costs.
10. Ignore any opinion that doesn't enhance your life. It's just an opinion. It's not reality. It's only their version of what they see, and that's all it is.

Number 89

Discipline is one of the highest forms of self-love, but I find it is overlooked a lot.

It is quite literally telling yourself that you will delay instant gratification and comfort for better things to come in the future. A lot of people see self-love as spa days and a fancy coffee, but true self-love is how you manage yourself in the face of adversity and despair. It is being willing to recognize and go toe to toe with what really matters in life.

Be yourself and be who you can admire the most. True self-love is hard. It is the hardest, yet most rewarding thing you can ever do. It is something that we all can improve on and something that is imperative to finding our way. If you love yourself first, then you are able to love others to the best of your ability.

Number 90

To manifest what we want in life requires steadfast dedication. Be a reflection of what you would like to receive. If you want love, give love. If you want truth, be truthful. If you want respect, give respect and respect yourself. This is the golden rule. If you want to manifest a beautiful life, simply operate from your highest good. This high vibrational state will attract all that you need and more than you could ever imagine. It will send you on your way to your destination of your soul's eternal glory and the fulfillment of your destiny.

Number 91

Let's talk more about something that we probably don't realize will actually help us on our soul's path. What you put in your body is also fuel. What you fuel yourself with determines how good you're going to do at what you want to do. The fuel that you put in your body is what makes you strong and confident. Fruits, vegetables, vitamins, and all those other good things that you can put in your body will help you and your body. Your body is your temple, and it is also going to help propel you on your way to finding your soul's path. This is helpful in many ways. Your body wants and craves good food and in turn remains strong for you on this earth. What you feed your body in turn feeds your heart, mind, and soul.

Number 92

I realize this is something maybe most of us don't ever want to do. But every now and then, a good cry is justified. Remember it's a form of release. Keeping things bottled up inside and held tight within us causes distress in our body. Anxiety, sleepless nights, and many different undesired outcomes can happen within our body if we don't release them. A good cry is therapeutic and can help you. Don't ever think that crying is a sign of weakness—it is not. Crying is letting go of the sadness within our body and soul. It is an escape from unwanted emotions. Let it out as it's a cleansing for ourselves. A cleansing allows for clarity. Clarity allows for peace and harmony in our soul and thus our path.

Number 93

Your soul deserves more peace.

Your soul deserves your patience.

Your soul deserves your time and energy.

Your soul deserves your love.

Your soul deserves to know its worth.

Your soul deserves its destined path.

Your soul deserves you to pay attention and listen.

Your soul deserves what it craves in this lifetime!

Your soul deserves everything in your power to make it feel safe and secure in knowing you will never let it down. Do not ever deny your soul anything it requires. You just know all what this entails for you. You will just know.

Number 94

Remember I said to keep it simple and just do the simple things in life. I like the acronym KISS: it means "Keep it simple, stupid!" Sorry, silly humor at its worst. We need to laugh at ourselves as it is very therapeutic. Just plain and simple breathing is very underrated, and it's also very powerful. Let's give it a try right now. Breathe in for six seconds, hold for six seconds, and breathe out for six seconds through your mouth. Do three cleansing breaths. Try it right now.

Breathe in . . . and flush it all out.

While breathing, remember that you're worthy of a beautiful life.

Remember that you are not the negative thoughts, but the beautiful empowering ones that reflect all your light.

You are a magnetic force, capable of achieving anything you can imagine.

Breathe in and out and free yourself from any energy that was preventing you from remembering your power.

And so it is . . . Just breathe!

Number 95

Let's talk about who we let in our lives. Let people teach you where they should fall into your life. People's actions will always speak louder than words. Let's set a table for you. Be very conscious of who you let sit at your table. Do they deserve a seat at your table? Do they deserve you? People that are allowed in your life have to be supportive and caring of you and conscious of your feelings. People in your life have to be genuinely happy for you and all that you do and all that you want to be in your life. Don't ever let anyone hold you back in your life. Sometimes people can have a bigger impact on our soul's journey of success than we realize. Please make sure that anyone allowed in your life is there for the right reasons. People in your life should always energize you and not exhaust you. You take on their energy, so make sure you vibe with your own energetic tribe.

Number 96

As we already talked about, you don't have to follow in the footsteps of everyone else. This is important, and I can't stress it enough. Each and every person is on a different path. Some people's destinations may be the same, but they will never take the same route. Some roads will be rocky; others a little smoother. Ultimately, as long as you focus on the path that you wish to take, no one else's will matter. Do not concern yourself with what others are doing on their path. Yours will be a completely different path that is predestined just for you. Once you stop comparing yourself to others and focus on only yourself, it is then you will find your way.

Number 97

Sometimes you need to remind yourself that you were the one who carried yourself through all your heartache. You're the one who sits with your body when it's sad and picks it right back up after. You are the one who feeds, clothes, and tucks yourself into bed. You have the strength to lovingly take care of yourself when it feels like the world is bleeding you dry. You have all the love you could ever need right inside of you right now. You are complete, deserving, worthy, and good enough right now! Once you know this and it is hardwired in your brain, you are well on your way to finding your soul's journey. I will keep telling you this until it is your natural state of being and you believe it wholeheartedly.

Number 98

I think it's important to remember that when you make life-altering decisions, it's normal to feel sadness, pressure, and confusion afterward. Change is hard and can bring up all kinds of feelings. Feeling this way does not mean you made the wrong decision. It just means that you need some time to readjust. Trust yourself and trust your decision. Then move forward to the next step in your journey for you. Remember a diamond is formed under pressure, and through this pressure, change is also created. You can create one of the most magnificent wonders of the world through pressure and change—a rare diamond. You are that magnificent wonder . . . You truly are! A diamond is about to be formed, while others are out collecting common stones.

Number 99

All of us do not escape this lifetime without experiencing pain and very tough lessons in life. We use this pain to become stronger and better, and this is growth.

The key to growth is to keep believing in yourself. Don't be fooled by that negative voice in your head—that voice that constantly tells you something negative that isn't even true.

Keep believing in your potential, intuition, ability to beat obstacles, and instincts on how to move forward. The same strength you have used to come this far is what is going to take you even further than you can imagine. It will take you as far as you want to go. It is limitless, so don't ever limit yourself. When we live with limitation, we don't go beyond what we considered possible for ourselves. Reach for the stars, beautiful, as you are one!

Number 100

Your energy is like gold. So let's consider it to be currency, shall we? When you "pay" attention to something, you're buying an experience. It's an investment, so "spend" carefully and only on things that will bring you a good return. Be selective. Be precise. Treat your time and energy wisely and with as much care as your finances and other valuable possessions. They're equally as valuable. I believe they are even more valuable as without them, you have no vitality for life or furtherance on your soul's path.

Number 101

Remember you can start late, start over, lose it all, fail again and again, yet still succeed. In life, age is just a number, and it is never ever too late to be something you want to be—and I mean *never*! Do not let life pass you by to the point that you're scared to take risks and do the things that you want to accomplish in life. It is possible at any age—just like you, at any age, can finally determine that you want to go on or continue on your soul's journey and still have it all. It is never too late! If you are still on this earth breathing, it is not too late! Even if you don't know where to begin, just take one step forward, one step after the other, and don't stop. I believe in you, and so should you. Each step you take and continue to take forward is a step in the right direction of finding your soul's purpose.

Number 102

Normalize being okay with letting people think whatever they want about you. Remember what other people think about you is none of your business, nor should you care. The idea that we're going to be liked, validated, or approved of by everyone is an illusion. Our mental health, peace, and happiness are more important than other people's acceptance, opinions, or perceptions of us. Mental well-being and self-esteem are vital to the success of fulfilling your soul's desires and purpose. You must like yourself at the end of each day, and if you do, that's all that matters.

Number 103

Let's get in this mindset: Not everything or everyone you lose is a loss. Some people and things are meant to be in your life for only a season. They're there to teach and show you things for you to realize life lessons. Just because you lose them or things in life, please remember they're not always a loss. They did serve a purpose, they did have meaning, and they were not by coincidence. These things progress you along your soul's journey. No reason to be sad about things that are in fact not a loss. They are life lessons that you needed to further you down your path. It can never be a loss when you win! In the long run, you do win even if you don't see it at first, my dear one.

Number 104

Real growth and power is when you start checking and correcting yourself instead of blaming others. Shifting blame is so easy to do. But let's be real and keep it at our core as we are responsible for ourselves and no one else. You take your power back by being responsible for your own life. You are always solely responsible for your life and your life's journey . . . 100 percent. Do not ever blame others for not being where you want to be. If you are not where you want to be, you have to only look at yourself in the mirror and say, "Let's do this . . . I am tired of being here. I want more out of life!" Go get it, my dear! What are you waiting for?

Number 105

I bet you can relate to this as I sure can.

You survived way too many storms to be bothered by mere raindrops, my dear. So there are little bumps in the road. So there are little obstacles that you didn't see coming. Are these going to keep you off your path? Are these going to keep you from trying? Are these going to derail you from ever fulfilling all your heart's and soul's desires? I think not, beautiful! You are too strong for that, as am I. Don't let things get you down or keep you down. They are only temporary, and more often than not, they are created by your mind and only an illusion. Once it passes, it's gone. I'd like to repeat the saying "This too shall pass." Let it pass and then continue on following your journey.

Number 106

This may sound kind of funny, but always set your vision higher than you can see. You may ask and wonder how to do this exactly. We always relish in our own limitations of what we think is achievable and obtainable for us. Take, for example, the simple request "Can I have a coffee?" This request is deemed very simple from previous conditioning. In your mind, we already know we will get the coffee. "Can I have $1 million?" Why, yes, you can! The very same law that got you the coffee will get you the million dollars. You just have to believe. Do you believe anything is possible? If you do, you are well on your way to discovering your soul's purpose, and it'll be something far greater than you ever expected it could be. You just have to believe and let the universe show you how good it can get! Actually, ask the universe and say, "Show me how good it can get!" Then sit back and watch what happens right before your eyes.

Number 107

Do you listen to your soul? Remember we talked about sitting in silence and just listening as a form of healing and what to do next comes to us in silence.

Your soul is leading you away from what is no longer good for you. Something that is meant for you will be peaceful, calm, and happy. Something that is not meant for you or your soul will be chaos and toxic.

Everything is aligning. Trust it. What you want wants you even more. What you desire desires you even more. What you seek seeks you even more.

Number 108

I feel these five things are very important but sometimes overlooked. They are five very influential things to do when you're trying to find your soul's purpose.

1. Your intuition never deceives you. Trust it without fail. Always trust your gut instinct.

2. Know the difference between your intuition and reality. A truth untold is a reality that never occurred. It is an illusion.

3. You have a limit to the amount of negative energy that you can take. That limit is different for everyone. As you become more pure of heart, it lessens greatly. Isolate and cleanse when needed.

4. Separate your emotions from the emotions of those you interact with. Don't let others seep their emotions into you. You will feel drained and exhausted if you do this.

5. You are a beaming light tower that guides others away from the darkness, yet you remain in the dark where they found you. The best way to heal is to be the light for someone else. But you also have to be your own light before you can light someone else's path. Light yourself first and then spread and shine it on others.

Number 109

Your story is not finished yet. The very best chapters are yet to come and be written.

You'll soon laugh in the places you have cried. Be still. When you are sad or have worries, ask yourself again, "Will I care about this in six months or a year?" If the answer is no, then don't give it any care or attention now. It is robbing you of the freedom of now. It is not relevant to your life, and you are wasting your valuable energy and time on something that doesn't deserve that much attention. We must learn how to decipher this and allot our time accordingly to what matters in life.

Number 110

To be vulnerable is very hard for some people. Some people will not let others see them vulnerable at all costs. It's like being in a new relationship and going forward in that relationship toward intimacy.

I read this before, and I loved it. It is said that the word "intimacy" means "into me see," suggesting that intimacy is allowing yourself to be seen. But only by knowing and accepting yourself fully can you then allow someone else to "see" you and be able to "see" them in return.

A step further is then allowing them to see into your soul. You must allow yourself to be vulnerable at times. This is when you are vulnerable enough to see all there is to see, and you may even discover something about yourself. In vulnerability, there is beauty, grace, and discovery, which in turn can further you down your soul's journey.

Number 111

Here we are . . . We made it!

The number 111 represents that you are on the right path!

Number 111 is a very strong manifestation number. When you see this number, your guides are reminding you that your mind is rapidly manifesting your thoughts quickly!

This is a huge sign to keep your thoughts positive and your mind clear because whatever you think will manifest into reality. Use your inner wisdom and intuition to guide you.

Please pay attention to your thoughts and keep an optimistic attitude toward your goals and dreams! When you see 111, take it as confirmation that you're manifesting your thoughts.

Thoughts always become things. There is not a thought placed in your heart that will be planted if it's not going to be seen to fruition. So have faith in that and be patient. It will be done. So from now on, whenever you see 111, you will know that you are on your destined path.

111 Ways to Finding your Soul's Purpose

Here are 111 thoughts to create your predestined reality.

The universe doesn't give you the people you want. It gives you the people you *need*—to help you, to hurt you, to leave you, to love you, and to make you the person you were meant to be.

Every person we meet in our lifetime means something and has a divine purpose—a purpose that propels us on our soul's journey. So the universe is never punishing you. It is giving you exactly what you need. Remember, in the universe, you are exactly where you need to be at any moment of time. Never question it. You are always exactly where you need to be. In times, it may not appear to be what you want. But trust me, it's what you need and where you belong. Having faith in this guidance is all you need.

You may find redundancy in this book as this is my very point. There may be only so many ways to truly discover one soul's path. But with every way that you choose to follow that path, you can make infinite discoveries. We know that no two of us are the same nor is the way that we go about finding our soul's path and journey. Let the uniqueness of your precious soul lead the way.

To me, this journey can be described only as ethereal. Like the warmth of the sun in winter, this journey is full of apricity—exquisitely beautiful and brilliant as each journey is as uniquely different as each beautiful soul that is created out of love. When you have your epiphany and discover your soul's purpose for yourself, it is completely and utterly euphoric and ineffable. Be in the state of eudaemonia, which implies a positive and divine state of being that all humanity is able to strive toward and hopefully reach. This can help to achieve your soul's glorious purpose.

Live well, live long, and live free, my dearest soul. Live to discover your dreams and aspirations in this crazy journey called life. I am proud of you. Imagine if we could all, one person at a time, simultaneously discover our soul's purpose. What a wonderful life and world we would live in for us all to behold and enjoy! Go write that next chapter of your life now.

Manufactured by Amazon.ca
Acheson, AB